Mindset of Highly Effective People

Change Your Habits – Change Your Life

Frederick Douglas

Table of Contents

1. Mindset Analysis
2. How To Have the Mindset for Success
3. Mindset and Depression
4. How Changing Your Mindset Can Change Your Life
5. Change Your Habits and Win
6. The A-Z Attributes of Highly Effective People
7. 8 Habits of Highly Effective People

Chapter I

Mindset Analysis

Suppose there is a glass. It is half full or empty with water. If we take a small survey and ask about the water situation in the glass, there would be two true answers:

- glass is half full with water,
- glass is half empty with no water.

It is said that the group of persons mentioning it half full are optimist or have positive mindset; on the other hand, the other group is pessimist or have negative mindset. Both statements are true or scientific. The positive or negative mindset is indicated when a person delivers a statement about or respond with some predictable exactness / exaggeration.

A mindset refers to a framework of intentions, perceptions, and emotions held by a person that predetermines a person's response to and interpretation of situations.

Negativity Traps

We take a few real life situations to fully grasp the concept and the characteristics that make up a negative or positive mindset:

1. A person faces a new situation/person and takes it with doubts without any scientific basis; it is indication of negative mindset. The other examples of doubtful mindset are - doubt about personal strengths, expect failures, and doubt on ground realities.

2. A person faces a novel situation/person and loose mental stability and responds with volatile attitude; it is indication of negative mindset. The other examples of volatile mindset are - lethargic response, impatient behavior, lousy decision making.

3. A person faces an unfavorable situation/person and loose self control and responds with anger; it is indication of negative mindset. The other examples of unjust mindset are - under or over estimations of abilities, excessive criticism on mistakes, and mild response on blunders.

4. A person faces a surprised situation/person and feels envy but responds with jealousy. It is a indication of negative mindset. The other examples of jealous mindset are - happy response on someone's miseries, sad feelings on someone's success, & defamation of opponent.

5. A person faces a disliked situation/person and responds proudly without any scientific basis. The other examples of proud mindset are - perfectionist approach, slavery of habits, and dictatorial stance during decision making.

6. A person faces an unexpected situation/person and considers it a threat without any scientific basis. The other examples of fearful mindset are - fear of future, fear of criticism, and fear of failure.

7. A person faces a new situation/person and feels frustration and respond with grief sentiments. The other examples of grief mindset are - overwhelmingly critical behavior, pessimism, and disbelief on real success.

These examples indicated seven major negativity traps or vicious circles of mental framework that make up a negative mindset. The solution to avoid the vicious traps is to develop a mental framework with positive intentions, positive perceptions, and positive emotions.

Mind Anatomy

Human mind has two sides - left and right. The left side is logical, analytical, and critical. On the other hand, the right side is intuitive, creative and synthetic. The left side is problem seeker while the right side is problem solver. Both sides have their own importance and significance.

In addition, we have two levels of mind - conscious and subconscious. The subconscious mind is filled with energy and power to accomplish multiple insurmountable tasks but is led by our conscious mind.

Conscious mind makes selection from continuous stream of thoughts (negative & positive) and develop a working pattern or belief system for subconscious mind. It is a continuous process of selection and execution in everyone's life.

Unfortunately, negative thoughts have a tendency to flit into our conscious mind. It involves left side of mind turning down the right side of the mind, do their damage and then flit back to continuous stream of thoughts. The significance of process is generally unnoticed.

In addition, we hardly perceive them as negative thoughts; we do not challenge them properly so that they may reside in our mind and can distort our mental framework, now and then.

Fortunately, the same process is with positive thoughts. They blink in our conscious mind, involve both sides of mind, without letting down any side of mind, do their constructive work and flew back to thought stream.

It is hard to notice them and to harness for permanent constructive activity. By noticing, captivating, maintaining, and protecting a positive thought, we can make them a permanent part of our mental framework for everlasting fruitful results.

Mindset is combination of intentions, perceptions and emotions. It has three powers for execution, will power, intellect power, and emotional power. These powers are essential ingredients of our mind. Equilibrium is necessary for the stability of mind pyramid; however, equilibrium may be wise or positive and unwise or negative.

Mindset Development - Self Suggestion

We have learned the mind anatomy with negativity traps that make our life miserable and unhappy. We can now move towards positive mindset. To avoid negativity traps, self suggestion is considered the best technique for mindset development. The words and phrases of self-suggestion should be real, constructive, energetic and dynamic. By continuous repetition we can make a positive image of our self.

- Any right effort with right intent and methods will produce good results.

- There is no real/permanent threat only opportunities.
- Any misery has blessing in disguise.
- Success is not pursued, it is attracted.
- Gratitude brings benefits.

Any positive suggestion is reacted by negative suggestion. A war is started in mind about these self suggestions with negative suggestions.

A negative belief produces or breeds new negative beliefs and a negative belief system is developed. A negative belief system plays havoc with an individual or system or society. A scientific / factual approach is strictly needed to avoid a negative belief system.

There are two tested weapons for negative suggestions - Knowledge and Wisdom. Knowledge is a weapon used at conceptual level to counter negative suggestions/beliefs, while, the wisdom is applied at practical level.

A suggestion based on knowledge and wisdom would be free from negativity traps. It is noteworthy that a rational person can make errors but not systematic errors. We learn from past errors / other's errors and adjust our beliefs and actions accordingly.

Example

We take an example from socio-economic life to establish and internalize the whole concept. It is three steps road map towards positive mindset - Thought Awareness, Rational Limitation, and Self Suggestions.

Step - I (Thought Awareness)

Suppose you are going for some presentation/negotiation. There are some typical negative thoughts you might experience about presentation /negotiation:

- Fear about the quality of performance, technical problems that may come up, and harsh criticism;
- Worry about the reaction of peers, general audience, and stakeholders;
- Doubt on real strengths/potential opportunities,
- Visualizing the negative consequences of a poor performance;
- Self-criticism over less than perfect preparation, rehearsal and practice,
- Frustration or Anger on certain real inadequacies or deficiencies.

These negative thoughts/negativity traps can damage confidence, harm performance, paralyze mental skills, and radiates negativity.

Step - II (Rational Limitations)

In rational limitation process you challenge the negative thoughts and counter them with rationality. Looking at some of the examples, the following challenges could be made to these common negative thoughts:

- Quality of performance: Have you gathered the information you need and prepared it properly for the event? Have you conducted a reasonable number of rehearsals, real or mental? If so, you've done as much as you can to give a good performance.

- Technical Problems and issues outside your control: The key to develop a rational limitation for successful presentation / negotiation on technical problems is to realize that you cannot control all relevant factors in your presentation/negotiation that may create a distraction. While you can control your own behavior or your organizational skills, you cannot control traffic jams, airline delays, power shutdown, computer network outrage, and communication problems due to damaged equipment. However, it is important to consider the possible risks and necessary steps to mitigate their effects.

- Fear about harsh criticism/ Worry about other people's reaction: If you perform the best you can, then you have given a good performance, fair people are likely to respond well. If people are not fair, then the best thing is to ignore them and rise above any unfair comments.

- Problems during practice: If some of your practices were less than perfect, then remind yourself that the purpose of practice is to identify problems so that they will not be repeated during the performance. Similarly, ask yourself whether it is reasonable to expect perfect performance. All that is important is effective/great performance not perfect.

Step - III (Self Suggestions)

By now, you would be more positive. The final step for effective positive mindset is to prepare self-suggestions to counter any remaining negativity. Continuing with the same example, some positive affirmations could be:

- Quality of performance: "I have prepared well and have rehearsed thoroughly. I am ready to give an excellent performance."

- Problems of distraction and issues outside your control: "I have thought everything that might reasonably happen and have planned how I can handle all likely contingencies. I am well equipped to react flexibly to any surprised situation."

- Worry about other people's reaction: "Fair people will react reasonably to a well-prepared performance. I will rise above any unfair criticism in a mature and professional way."

Chapter II

How To Have The Mindset For Success

Learning how to have the mindset for success is crucial when you want a successful and blissful life. If you are like me, you might have many goals you want to achieve. Whatever these goals are, the key is to have a growth mindset rather than a fixed one. But what is the difference and how you get it?

How can you set and have the mindset for success? Do you want to reach your goals more rapidly? In how many years did you plan to achieve your goals?

Many people, as well as I, preach hard work, focus, persistence and more but these are by-products of something else. It is something much more powerful than we can all develop. This extraordinary thing is critical to success, and it is your mindset.

Without the right mindset, you might find yourself sidetracked by your everyday routine. You can also often be distracted by the latest and most fabulous idea you are just having, which rarely pushes you to follow one path until successful.

You may think that you have all the time in the world to achieve your goals. But you have to realize that if you set your mindset for success, you can apply it to other domains as well. This way, you will reach your goals much faster and find yourself with the capacity to possibly form new and bigger goals.

The Trap of the Mindset

It is always better to fail many times before succeeding as it will help you avoid many of the psychological traps. One of the key traps is to believe that you are smarter than other people, or that you do not have to work hard because you have talent, or that you have nothing to learn.

To have the right mindset to be successful in life, you do not need to have extraordinary intelligence or be gifted with talents.

The moment you believe that success is determined by an ingrained level of ability, you will brittle in the face of adversity.

So, as soon as you think success is determined by talent, you become weak when you have to face obstacles.

The Difference between a Fixed and Growth Mindset

So as soon as people see intelligence or abilities as fixed, they believe that many things are impossible for them to achieve because they put limits on themselves and their skills. And that is what is called a fixed mindset.

But other persons see abilities as qualities that can be developed which is, in this case, called a growth mindset. The important part is that those two different frames of mind lead to not the same behaviors and results.

When you have a growth mindset, you know you can change your intelligence, and increase your aptitudes and skills over time. But people with a fixed mindset do not think it is possible. So, the difference between the two groups is the perspective on intellect and brainpower.

The Possibility of a Different Mindset

Many studies have shown similar effects for the mindset about any ability such as problem-solving, playing sports, managing people or anything else you would like. The key to success is not merely effort, focus or resilience, but it is the growth mindset that creates them.

Your mindset is critical. When you directly are trying to build determination or persistence, it is not nearly as effective as if as addressing the mind frame that underlies these traits. How many people think of themselves as not creative people, or sociable, or math oriented, or even athletic?

On the other hand, some people may think that they are naturals. But if you want to fulfill your full potential, you need to start thinking differently. You have to realize that you are not chained to your current capabilities and that you can modify your mindset.

A Mindset Can Be Changed

People like Charles Darwin, Marcel Proust, and many others along with all high achievers such as Mozart to Einstein built their abilities. But the vital thing here is to realize that you can change your ability and picture yourself where you want to be. When you have a growth mindset, you bring your game to new levels. So, how does a growth frame of mind do that?

Well, there are biological manifestations to mindset. Tests show that with people who have a fixed mindset, the brain becomes most active when they receive information about how they perform. Whereas people with a growth mindset, they have their mind being most active when they receive information about what they could do better next time.

In other words, people with a fixed frame of mind worry the most about how they are judged while those with a growth mindset focus the most on learning. A fixed mind sees effort as a bad thing, something that only people with low capabilities need while those with a growth approach see effort as what makes them smart and as a way to grow.

And when they hit a setback or failure, people with a fixed mindset tend to conclude that they are incapable, so to protect their ego, they lose interest or withdraw. It is often taken as a lack of motivation, but behind it is a fixed frame of mind.

Whereas, people with a growth frame of mind believe that setbacks are a part of personal development. They find a way around the problem, so it means that you have to challenge yourself, but it also says that you have to praise yourself for being great at something or being smart.

Mindset Affects Everything

Trying hard pushes you to work even harder next time you face a challenge. Do not get into the fixed mindset of thinking that when you win, you are a winner and when you lose, it must make you a loser. The reason being is that your mindset affects your performance.

Remember that you can change your mindset any time you wish. And that is important because many people have a fixed mind frame about something or another. When you teach or have a growth mindset, not only it improves you , but it also narrows down the achievement gap.

Mindset affects all of us. In the workplace, managers and supervisors with a fixed mindset do not accept feedback as much, and they do not mentor people. A wrong or right frame of mind even touches relationships, sports, and health.

Why do schools not teach the growth mindset to children rather than being so critical?

Tips to Have the Mindset for Success

- Get a growth mindset.
- Develop Success Habits.
- Recognize that a growth mindset is beneficial.
- Know that your brain changes when you work hard to improve yourself.
- Make a small step toward each of your goals each day.
- Learn how to develop your abilities as well as teaching others.
- Capture all of the information that could help you.
- Do a deliberate daily practice to develop your abilities through effective effort.
- Listen to audio books or learn a new language on your phone while you are out for a walk rather than music.
- Clip articles and inspiring ideas for a vision board.
- Learn from your failures by asking yourself what you learned from the experience.
- Know your strengths and weaknesses.
- Develop core skills that will help you reach and achieve your goals.

After experiencing a setback, do not dwell on it. Instead, make an evaluation, and move on to the next thing.

And so, learn that to have a right mindset will allow you to succeed beyond all your expectations. You have to learn to talk back with a growth mindset voice when you listen and hear your fixed mind frame. Therefore, when you hear it say "You can't," just add another word to it which is "Yet."

Chapter III

Mindset And Depression

Mindset and depression are closely linked by the ability of the mindset you have to expand or contract your life.

The view you have of yourself has an overwhelming influence on the way you live your life and this is often a difficult concept to grasp when you are depressed. Simply acknowledging this concept and doing something about it are worlds apart.

Thought patterns can affect the way we feel each day and to control this, there is a need to question where negative thoughts come from. Questions to answer can include:

"I constantly limit myself. Where did I learn these beliefs?"

"When did I take on this type of thinking pattern?"

"At what time in my life did I begin the downhill slide I'm on now?"

"I don't like the person I've become. When did this happen?"

"How did I get to the place I am in now?"

Understanding Mindset

Our state of mind and behavior is greatly influenced by our thoughts even though we know that our thoughts are not who we are as individuals. Our behavior is such that it corroborates the negative thoughts that we have. Depression is a state of mind and it is not who we are as a person. What I mean by this is: we are not a 'depressed person', we are in a 'state of depression'. Changing depressive thoughts patterns that have been developing, often over many years, to overcome depression takes commitment and determination.

There are two types of Mindset - "Growth" and "Fixed".

Fixed Mindset

"Fixed Mindset" is the belief that your qualities at birth are carved in stone. That the intelligence you have now and your moral character is what you will have for the rest of your life. Learning and growing are not part of the 'fixed mindset' way of thinking.

Many of us are trained in a fixed mindset early on in life, often unwittingly by those who care the most about us. Caregivers and educators that we come across in our school years may believe that the IQ and EQ we have initially in school are fixed and as such treat us as though we have no capacity to improve.

In our early school years we don't like to be seen as stupid or unintelligent so we instinctively act to look smart. The outcome of this is that we fail to learn to take risks for fear of being 'exposed' as not being very smart. The enjoyment of learning and investigating new things are lost through fear of failing.

The behavior of 'proving ourselves' repeats itself throughout our lives whether it be in relationships, our careers or leaning institutions as we feel we are being continually judged.

This type of repetitive behavior is potentially devastating to our development.

Growth Mindset

"Growth Mindset" in contrast, is based on the belief that your basic qualities are just the starting point for development. You have the ability to learn, grow and cultivate whatever initial gifts, skills, interests or disposition you have been given.

If you have a 'growth mindset' you have the opinion that each one of us has the opportunity to change and grow through practice and the implementation of developmental exercises. Your potential at any given time or in any circumstance is unknown.

Now the uncertainty of any given situation is part of the process of growing. In children and adults with a 'growth mindset' a love of learning can be created at any stage in their development.

No longer does an individual feel the need to 'prove' themselves as they believe that they are always on a learning curve and that any setback is just part of that learning process.

Mindset And Depression

As I mentioned at the start, the type of mindset we have can influence whether we are prone to depression or not and one of the tools at our disposal is that of changing our mindset.

In different areas of our lives, out mindset may vary. Unfortunately, if you are struggling to overcome depression, it is likely that the "Fixed Mindset" is pervasive throughout most of your thinking.

How To Create A Productive Mindset

When it comes to creating a productive mindset lot of us have a hard time. Most people get into procrastination mode, which is usually an easier choice by putting off what needs to be started.

But what is a productive mindset? And what occurs when your intentions to get things done are crumbling? How does it happen? What can you do to focus on what is essential to your progress?

We all have experienced this before. I am no stranger to it. You have the feeling like you are running around and being busy all the time. You spend all day working and doing things, but at the end of the day, you look back and realize that you have done very little. It appears that of the ten different tasks you wanted to complete, you achieved only two or three of them.

Well, it often happens because of your mindset not being established in the right way. To have a productive mindset is to make the best use of your combined resources, time, energy, and efforts. Being productive is something you and I strive to realize.

I said it numerous times in other articles but let me repeat it; your mindset is everything. It is the groundwork for every achievement, victory, and success in your life. So, it is necessary for you to cultivate a productive mindset. If I am saying this, it is because if you want to reach your goals, you need to create a mind that is efficient.

First Steps to a Productive Mindset

As you know, each of us is different, so it is quite important that you structure your day in a way that works for you. First of all, you should observe your daily routine and be honest with yourself by examining if you do have a productive mindset or if you are just being busy.

To be productive means that you have a clear mind and are focused on what you want to accomplish. It also means that you are using all of your resources to achieve your goals profitably. The next step involves morning habits that would help you get more done throughout the day.

To continue creating a productive mindset, you have to choose which vital assignment to start first when you sit down for work. You have to make the right choices so you can kick off your day with dynamic momentum.

Primary Elements of a Productive Mindset

How productive your mindset often begins with your thoughts and habits. You always must start your day by being grateful for what is about to start. Always be ready for possibilities. Plans often change or get rescheduled leaving you with some free time.

Rather than being upset about it or feeling let down, use this time to read a chapter of a book, or listen to an audiobook. Each afternoon, I walk for two hours and during that time I hear some audiobook to educate myself.

You must have the willingness to know and learn new things. And it is also a great way to get your day back on track. But let me show you some of the primary elements of a productive mindset.

Vision and the Productive Mindset

You have to picture what you want and visualize it. It helps you focus and gives you an ideal image of what the outcome could look like. Without a picture in your mind, it is quite challenging to have the productive mindset to achieve a goal. People with a vision can accomplish what seems impossible.

Inspire Your Frame of Mind

You have to cultivate and motivate your mindset for it to be productive. Without motivation or inspiration, there is nothing to drive you to set goals. Inaction and procrastination destroys any improvements you wish to make or dreams you want to achieve.

Self-confidence is a Mindset

You have to believe that you are capable of doing what you set your mind to do. Self-confidence can help you reach your full potential and a more productive mindset. Stress is a natural reaction, so you have to relax by taking a deep breath and a small reflective pause. Then refocus on the day ahead. It will give you greater confidence.

Methods for a Prolific Mindset

In today's world, our mind runs through a list of dozens of things simultaneously. Some of those things keep us living in the future, while memories, good or bad, retain us in the past. Yet, to create a productive mindset is to live in the beauty of the present.

Be in the present. Focus and fully engage in whatever essential task you have to assure and put your best work forward. Here are some essential productivity methods to create a prolific mindset.

Having Positive Outlook

In creating a productive mindset, your attitude has to be positive rather than negative, because it can make you or break you. When you have a positive outlook, it allows room for opportunity and option, while having a negative attitude defeat your frame of mind before you even begin.

A Productive Mindset is Being Persistent

Most of us know that the path to success does not come easily. So, you have to be persistent and willing to overcome any barrier or adversity coming your way. Push yourself beyond your limits and persist to achieve your goals. Do not let setbacks, circumstances, or even the opinions of others influence your actions and your determination to become successful.

Refreshing Your Mindset

To experience a productive mindset, you have to be at your best. That means you have to take care of yourself. Getting some rest and enough sleep each night is essential. You have to eat right and give yourself a few small breaks during the day. And you should always be aware of how you feel.

Tips to Create a Productive Mindset

- Write a to-do list for the day the night before. It will help you keep focusing on what you need to get done so that you will have a more productive mindset.

- Get enough sleep, because if you do not, your fatigue will eat away at your productivity. A lack of sleep has an apparent impact on any mental performance.

- Be motivated as it is a crucial element in working towards your goals. You need to have something that is pulling you towards achieving the success you want in life.

- Start your work with the most essential task. It is an excellent approach if you have the discipline to see to it.

- Cultivate the persistence to keep going, even when it is hard. To be persistent and never giving up is essential to any long-term success.

- Always hold a mental picture of the vision of the life that you want for yourself. It is that vision that will guide you and help you to create a more productive mindset through your day.

- Control your attitude and how you feel about things, no matter the circumstances. Even if you feel like you cannot control outside factors, you should positively view everything as it is an absolute necessity.

- Create a routine that helps you awaken your brain and mind, give you motivation and shows you a clear picture of your vision.

- Have an evening routine. Following the same ritual every evening, such as making yourself a caffeine-free hot drink, brushing your teeth, then dressing for bed, helps you get into the right state of mind for sleep.

- Take time to regenerate, recharge and refresh. That way, you will always keep a productive mindset.

Chapter IV

How Changing Your Mindset Can Change Your Life

If you have been struggling to lose weight, improve a relationship, find a new job or just have more fun, the answer may be in your mindset.

Mindset is a concept developed over a decade ago to understand how people cope with failures. Mindset is the view we adopt of ourselves and to prove that it can profoundly affect how we live our lives.

People generally fall into two categories, those with a fixed mindset and those with a growth mindset. A "fixed" mindset suggests that our intelligence, ability and personality are carved in stone and do not change much over our lifetime.

An example of this mindset might be "I am not athletic"" or "I am a math person" which suggest that these traits can't change. The downside to a "fixed" mindset is these kinds of beliefs limit personal growth.

By contrast, a "growth" mindset suggests that individuals have basic abilities but can develop and cultivate these and other abilities or intelligence and talents through effort and strategies. This view allows for potential to grow and opens us to greater possibility and success.

Adopting a growth mindset can improve all areas of life from personal to professional. Changing from a fixed mindset to a growth can be accomplished through three steps.

Three Steps to Grow Your Mindset

Growth mindset is based on the belief that we can change throughout our lifetime. While changing our beliefs can be challenging, the growth mindset can be developed in small steps.

Awareness of how we think. The first step is to become aware of our behavior. When we tune into our thoughts and start to notice our reaction to challenges, criticism and setbacks, we can notice patterns where we are stuck.

Challenges, criticism and setbacks are roadblocks with a fixed mindset. For example, a fixed mindset reaction to a difficult challenge is to question whether we can succeed. If we don't think we can, why would we try only to fail.

For instance, the thought "I am not going to volunteer to help my boss with that project because I am not sure I have all the skills. If I fail, I will look like a fool in front of my co-workers" is limiting the possibility for growth.

In addition, constructive criticism is taken as an affront and a typical "fixed" mindset response is to become defensive and feel like a failure. "I can't believe she told me my paper needed work. I am a horrible writer."

Setbacks can be a reason to give up because they reinforce our belief that we did not have the ability in the first place. "I auditioned and didn't get a part. I knew I wasn't a good singer."

Choice, The second step is to take this awareness and begin to see each of these is a choice. While it is comfortable to stay with our habitual responses, growth occurs when we make choices to change our limiting beliefs.

A limiting belief keeps us in a safe zone but also keeps us from growth. For example, if my limiting belief is "I can never lose weight because my parents were overweight", why try at all? This choice is to default to limiting thoughts. Or in the setback example of not being selected because of lack of natural ability, the response is a choice to give up because I "failed" and my ability is fixed.

The growth choice requires more effort to stretch our abilities or maybe change the strategy. Challenge the belief. T

he final step is to challenge the belief as it comes up. To challenge these beliefs, it is important to see challenges, criticism or setbacks as opportunity for growth.

For instance, in the above example of the audition "although I did not get this part, I learned about the audition process and I will continue to take voice lessons because it is important to me and I enjoy it. I might not get a part the next time but I will keep trying new strategies.

I can ask for feedback and see how I might improve." The shift from focusing solely on the result to enjoying the process is critical with a growth mindset.

In addition, being open to feedback helps us develop much more than seeing it as a failure. It suggests incorporating the phrase "I am not there yet" instead of "I failed" to stay encouraged and to keep trying. As Henry Ford said "whether you think you can or think you can't - you are right!"

Chapter V
Change Your Habits And Win

We are all creatures of habit. That is human nature. But when life gets busy, and it does, we can all fall into the trap of going nowhere, simply by habit.

If you want something different, you have to do something different. If you want things to be better, then you have to be better.

In a nutshell - nothing changes if nothing changes!

How often have you heard the expression "I'll be happy when... "

When what? When you have a new job, when you buy a new car, when you move into a new town, when you lose weight. The truth is, before you change any of those things, you need to change yourself.

You need to change your habits to win.

Self improvement is the key to success. Not money, not a career, not how big a house you own or what sports car you drive. True success comes from within, and once you master that, all the rest will follow, abundantly.

This is not to say you need to stop everything you are currently doing. The first and most important decision you need to make is a promise to your self.

Are you committed, passionate, confident, determined, enthusiastic, excited, organised and ready to act now? Then congratulations. You are ready to change your habits and win.

For so many of us, we stop learning and growing on a personal development level once we leave school. We get a job, start a family, and generally get caught up in life. But that is when it is so easy to fall into the habit trap. It happens to most of us as some time in our lives.

The important thing is once you become aware of it, do something about it. Don't sit back and hope it will change by itself. Remember, nothing changes if nothing changes.

In order to change your habits and win, you need to grow as a person. Success is not something that happens overnight. But it won't happen at all if you never start.

Self improvement is an awakening of yourself and your capabilities. Personal development will open the door to opportunities you never thought possible, and you will find you are capable of so much more than you ever gave yourself credit for.

Changing your habits to win a lifestyle of success is the beginning of a new direction that can only lead to a bigger and better future and who doesn't want that.

Simple Strategies to Change Your Habits

"Your beliefs become your thoughts,

Your thoughts become your words,

Your words become your actions,

Your actions become your habits,

Your habits become your values,

Your values become your destiny."

- Mahatma Gandhi

A large proportion of our daily actions are habits: routines that we've formed over a lifetime. It's estimated that about 40% of people's daily activities are habits. Some habits serve a positive purpose - such as locking the door when you leave the house, speaking with pleasantries during a phone conversation, or letting the dog out when he sits by the back door.

Most of us, however, have habits that we wish we could break. Many of which, revolve around food. Examples may be having something sweet in the afternoon to get you out of an energy slump, snacking at night when you're not hungry, or rewarding yourself with a second helping of dinner after a stressful day at work.

Habits, especially bad habits, are difficult to break. Breaking a habit takes a tremendous amount of willpower, and willpower is a limited resource. It's highest in the morning and is easily eroded by stress, fatigue, anxiety, happiness, or pretty much any emotion or situation.

It wavers when someone offers you a piece of chocolate, and admits defeat at the smell of fresh baked pie. It may put up a good fight at breakfast time; after all, most people find it relatively easy to say no to chocolate cake at 7am.

But even on a good day, you may find your willpower levels are pretty low by 3 or 4 in the afternoon. It leaves you vulnerable to the breadbasket at dinner, the handfuls of cereal after supper, or the chips after the kids are in bed.

Willpower is not the answer. So, instead of trying to break bad habits, aim to change them.

The lifecycle of a habit can be broken down into three parts; cue, routine and reward. For example, the cue to lock the door when leaving the house is, well, leaving the house. The routine is locking the door, and the reward is the peace of mind that your house and belongings are relatively safe.

In the example of the 2PM treat as a 'pick me up', the cue would be the feeling of wanting energy, feeling bored at work, or simply the fact that it's 2PM. The routine would be heading to the vending machine, office kitchen, or desk drawer in search of a candy bar or muffin. The reward would be the short-lived increase in energy, the pleasure of having something sweet on your tongue, and a break from work.

If you want to stop the sugar habit, simply saying "I am going to give up my afternoon treat" is likely not enough. When that cue hits, it's hard to resist! Your body needs something and up until this point you've been feeding it candy.

In order to swap a habit, you first need to pause and recognize that your actions are just that- a habit. Also, you must remember that you are in charge, and you have the power to change your habits.

Ask yourself the simple, but often emotional question "what do I really want?" Think about the reward- how do you want to feel? When that afternoon slump hits, you want something. But, do you really want that slightly stale doughnut or to wolf down a chocolate bar while sitting at your desk? Or, are you simply bored with the task you're working on and need a break? Do you need to feel re-energized? Do you need a pleasurable experience?

Next, think of different routines that could yield the same reward. If you are battling an energy slump and need to feel energized, would a short walk or doing a few squats to get the your blood flowing do the trick? Perhaps, a short visit with a co-worker to offer a change of scenery or a mind break? What about going outside for some fresh air, or taking a few minutes to stretch? If you are slightly hungry would a crisp, juicy apple do the trick?

What about the evening rummage through the pantry after your kids are in bed? Are you looking for a reward after a long, hard day? Are you bored? Are you stressed? Again ask, "what do I really want?" Do you need some excitement to overcome boredom? Do you just need to unwind? Would working on a project, indulging in an entertaining novel or writing in a journal give you what you really need?

To get started, pick one habit that you'd like to change. Identify the cue associated with the action, and the feeling that you get from the reward. Make a list of alternatives, more healthful habits you can engage in to replace that bad habit. Rehearse the situation in your mind and picture yourself engaging in that new habit. The more you practice, the better you'll get!

Although habits can most certainly be changed, the process is not always easy. Do not expect to change a habit overnight. It takes patience and persistence! Proceed with kindness, understanding and acceptance of yourself. Celebrate your successes and learn from your mistakes.

Top 3 Factors of Changing Your Habits and Realizing Your Goals

You Are Your Habits

We will explore some practical ways to change habits, and some factors that influence your ability to change habits.

But first, what exactly do we mean by habits?

Habits are simply those behaviors, thoughts, or actions that we do on a regular basis. Habits are largely unconscious: we do them without thinking or consciously choosing. While on the surface we may believe that we are consciously choosing each of our actions in daily life, the truth is that much of what we do is largely automatic.

It's a good thing that life is ruled largely by habitual tendencies, for if we had to consciously choose each behavior, we'd probably get stuck somewhere between the bedroom and the bathroom in the morning as we reinvented our morning routine each day.

While habits save time in most contexts of life, a downside to habits is when the behavior is something that is harmful to us. Whether abusing some substance, overspending, or harmful relationship patterns, habits can seriously limit our ability to experience happiness.

We all know what these habits are. You have a list of things that you'd like to change in your life... and you probably spend a lot of energy avoiding your list!

But if you're reading this, you probably have at least one tendency that you'd like to change. If you do, it's important to consider the following three factors that influence your ability to change your habits:

1. Crisis causes change

It could be a bona-fide catastrophe, or the sudden realization that things just can't continue the way they are. In the moment of crisis, we get an opportunity to change course dramatically as we look for a better way.

2. New peer group

When all your friends do one thing, you're likely to do the same. When you join a new peer group, you adopt new habits. When you look at your friends, what kind of habits do they reflect? If they are not the habits you want in your life, it may be time to upgrade your peer group.

3. Belief

Finally, belief is an important component of making changes. Significantly changing behavior requires a leap into the unknown. Where this belief in change ultimately comes from defies scientific reason, but is an essential ingredient in success.

These three factors interrelate. For example, suppose you want to start a new business, but you are stuck working at an office job and have no time to put into your business.

One day, your company downsizes and you have a financial and personal crisis. You have the opportunity to make a change as you reflect on your life and gain insight into what you really want in life:

your own business. You also have a new peer group as you are no longer surrounded by your old colleagues.

With any luck, you are surrounded by helpful friends or have found an online community to support your ideas. The new peer group and insight from the crisis supports your belief that you can create your own business.

Chapter VI

The A-Z Attributes of Highly Effective People

Effective people are known for being productive in all ramifications of life. They are successful and produce strong or favorable impression on people. They influence people positively and impart their generations. They follow certain principles and pay close attention to the following characteristics;

A - Aspiration

Aspiration is born out of AMBITION. It is a strong feeling or desire to be successful in life and to achieve great things.

B - Brilliance

You have to learn how to put your brain to use effectively. Being intellectual is built by absorbing useful resources and utilizing them to produce exceptional results.

C - Curiosity

The more questions you ask, the more answers you get and hence, the more knowledgeable you become. Your yearning for information and your eagerness to discover new things will keep you on the path of success.

D - Discipline

There is no successful person that has ever made it without discipline. Discipline is having a conscious control over your lifestyle. An attribute close to it is DILIGENCE which is persistence and hard work even in the face of challenges.

E - Excellence

This is the quality of being outstanding. This is an attribute successful people don't joke with. Being the best and standing out always and consistently. Excellence is not a trait, it is developed. This is the quality that distinguishes you. Your ability to outshine your contemporaries makes you unique and exceptional.

F - Focus

When your concentration on a particular thing is high, you can hardly miss any detail just like a properly focused beam of light. Having a TARGET and going for it with all your resources is an important key to effectiveness.

G - Growth

To be highly effective, know that success is not a destination but a journey. No matter where you attain in life, there is always room to do more. Refuse to be stagnated by your past glory and keep moving on. Keep growing!

H - Hard Work

You will agree with me that gold is not picked on the streets, neither is oil scooped by the river banks. If you want an exceptional result, then you must be willing to pay the price. You must dig, toil and perspire. Though hard work comes with pain and sacrifices, the gain thereof is immeasurable.

I - Integrity

If you trade your integrity for the smallest amount, then you are worth the cheapest commodity money can buy. Honesty may not put food on your table, but it will save your name. Do not soil your REPUTATION no matter the temptation.

J - Judiciousness

Successful people are good managers of time and resources. You must be prudent enough to maximize resources so as to avoid wasting them. You must be accountable for every action taken.

K - Knowledge

This is the most powerful tool needed to remain relevant in your generation. Seek it, find it and apply it. Every other thing may be stolen from you but a man who will steal your knowledge must be able to cease your breath first. Guide it jealously because KNOWLEDGE IS POWER.

L - Learning

Learning should be an endless process to remain productive. The day you stop learning, you start dying. Learning keeps you contemporary. Reading is one way of learning, as a matter of fact - READERS ARE LEADERS, so do not joke with your personal LIBRARY.

M - Motivation

Most successful people are self-motivated. You have to believe in yourself and in your dreams. There must be a drive from within that will fuel your passion for productivity.

N - Nobility

You need to possess an excellent moral character. Noble people are true to their words and they do whatever positive thing they determine to do. They exude a charisma that is worthy of emulation.

O - Optimism

You have to develop a positive attitude towards life and hold on to your hopes and expectations. Condition your mind to remain confident about the steps you take. It is the oil that will keep your lamp burning.

P - Purpose

A man of purpose is a man of VISION. When the purpose of a thing is not known, abuse is inevitable. Purpose defines your direction and keeps you focused on your desired goal.

Q - Quality

Highly effective people set standards for themselves that cannot be compromised. Everything about you should reflect your genuineness.

R - Resilience

When challenges come because they will definitely show up, your ability to exhibit courage in the face of obstacles guarantees your success story. You just have to the tough to approach the problems that life poses to you and seek ways to overcome them because you are a PROBLEM SOLVER. Never give up!

S - Sensitivity

Your response to your immediate environment and how you are being influenced by it depends on how sensitive you are. Changes will definitely occur but how you maneuver your way through them will determine your level of productivity.

T - Time Management

Only a fool thinks that he has all the time in the world to do whatever he likes. Effective people do not joke with their time because every moment is important and should be well accounted for.

U - Understanding

Your ability to comprehend issues and situations goes a long way to determine how effective you will be especially in the area of management of people. Your approach to life and living must reflect clairvoyance.

V - Value

Your value system is what projects your personality. It is what reveals the stuff you are made of. It shows who you are and what you stand for. Developing good values is inevitable for effective people.

W - Wisdom

Mere men can rule but only wise men can lead. Wisdom is not inherited; it is acquired over time through experiences. Effective people use this tool to approach life issues with a good sense of judgement.

X - Xtra-Ordinariness

Going the extra mile, taking the extra step and doing the extra thing differentiates effective people from ordinary men. You must be ready to BREAK RECORDS, set paces and establish your uniqueness.

Y - Yield

Effective people are result-oriented. They are interested in measuring their level of productivity at all times and challenging themselves to become better in all they do.

Z - Zeal

You must show great enthusiasm and optimism. You have to be proactive to get results that are worthy of commendation.

Chapter VII

8 Habits Of Highly Effective People

The dictionary defines effective as 'exerting influence' or 'capable of having a striking effect'. Almost all great people fall into this category. What does it take to be highly effective? Is it the same as being efficient? Many of us find that though we are the latter, our efforts are hardly recognized. So, if you have been struggling to become effective, here is a list of habits that you may consider imbibing.

The 8 Habits of Highly Effective People

People who are highly effective have certain qualities that are common. Here are a few you could cultivate:

1. **Be proactive:** Stephen R. Covey, in his highly influential bestseller 'The 7 habits of Highly Effective People', outlines the habits of such people. Being proactive tops the list. Whether it was Gandhi or Victor Frankl, who defied the horror of the Nazi death camps to become a great psychiatrist, effective people are undaunted by their environment. They decide the path they will take and follow it no matter what.

2. **Focus on the goal:** Whether it was Mother Teresa or Martin Luther King, they all started out with a goal. What is it that you wish to achieve in 10 or 20 years? Effective people have a goal before they start out. Once you are clear about the destination, you can build the steps you need to get there.

3. **Concentrate on the here and now:** Effective people have the habit of starting from where they are from the moment they have set their goals. Gandhi may have gone on to lead a nation to freedom, but he started out by realizing his ideals among a few Indians on a farm in South Africa. Effective people know the importance of putting first things first.

4. **Focus on the greatest good:** An important habit that goes much against effectiveness is the general tendency to think only of one's own victory or success. Effective people think of change not just for themselves but for all their fellowmen in similar circumstances.

5. **Stress on communication:** All effective people are great communicators, which includes being a good orator as well as a good listener. Stephen Covey referred to this as 'seek to understand, then to be understood.' Listen with empathy and note not just the meaning of the words but also the feeling underlying them.

6. **Constant self renewal:** Covey used the words 'sharpen the saw' to define this habit. A process of renewal and rejuvenation that nourishes your mental, physical and emotional powers is a must if you want to be effective. How can you have an impact if you yourself are tired and worn out?

7. **Respect for all:** The ability to synergize is the universally acknowledged habit that all effective people had. It means to incorporate each individual into the whole without losing sight of their individual differences.

8. **Go to the root cause**: If you wish to be effective you have to ask the question 'Why?'- not just once, but many times. Only then can you come to the root cause. Without uprooting this, you will find that the same problems recur.

Reflect on yourself and cultivate these habits to make yourself a highly effective person.

Conclusion

You want success, but you're not sure how to get there. It's actually quite simple. It's your mindset. Your mindset is the attitude that you have toward something.

And your mindset is the deciding factor in whether or not you'll actually achieve the success that you're looking for. You can have a negative or a positive mindset.

People who have negative attitudes usually see the reasons why something can't be achieved and these people are self-limiting when it comes to success. But people with positive mindsets see the problems in a task and look for ways to adapt around or through the problem to come up with a solution that works.

Mindset matters because with the right mindset, you'll be able to tap into the potential that you have for success. Everyone has this potential, but not everyone reaches for it. Those who do will experience personal and professional growth.

www.ingramcontent.com/pod-product-compliance
Lightning Source LLC
Chambersburg PA
CBHW080911220526
45466CB00011BA/3554